Fred Long
A Case of
LIBEL

by Nancy Richmond

An Interactive Book

Copyright 2021
All Rights Reserved

About The Author

Nancy Richmond is a retired Greenbrier County Judge. She is also an historian, a certified genealogist, a member of the Greenbrier Historical Society and the award winning author who has written more than thirty books. She has been a columnist for many newspapers and nationally syndicated magazines. Several of Richmond's historical biographies have been inducted by the Library of Congress into their Adams and Jefferson Historical Reading Rooms in Washington, DC; as well as into the National Library of the Sons of the American Revolution in Louisville, KY. Others have been made into audio books. Her volume, "Appalachian Folklore - Omens, Signs and Superstitions" is used in medical schools to introduce student doctors to the unique culture and heritage of the people of Appalachia. Nancy Richmond and her husband Charles currently reside in Historic Lewisburg, WV.

website: nancyrichmondbooks.com

Author's page : www.amazon.com>Nancy-Richmond

Contents

1. Introduction   1

2. Fred Long Commits Libel   5

3. Fred Long Claims Libel   27

4. Lawsuit Documentation   53

5. Bibliography   133

6. Case Notes   139

Introduction

Dear Reader:

This volume was written both as an example and as a precaution to anyone who reads it. In our society today, most books are online, people can post emails, videos and instagrams on social media and web sites that are read by millions of people in a single day. Comment sections are attached to almost every newspaper and commercial business online.

Libel is the publication in words, photos, pictures or symbols, of a false statement of fact that can harm another's reputation. Libel is now rampant in this country. Billions of dollars are being spent and thousands of lives are being ruined in America every year in libel court cases.

When I experienced just such an event in my life recently, I was shocked at how quickly I became entangled in the effort to clear my name and protect myself from totally untrue and undeserved libel. This book relates the events as they took place, and hopefully will be of help to others who have been or in the future will be falsely accused of libel. The surest prevention for such an allegation is this: Before any statement made about another person or organization can be proven to be libel in a court of law, that statement MUST BE FALSE. If what you say is true, it is not libel and it can be used in any context without fear of being sued. The right of freedom of speech is guaranteed in the United States Constitution. We also have the right to our own opinion, so a good rule of thumb is to begin any controversial comment by saying 'in my opinion' or 'I believe'.

In an effort to raise awareness of the libel crisis, I have modified this book to be interactive with my readers. You can follow the case, getting weekly updates, in my face book group 'Nancy Richmond Books', and make comments or suggestions for what actions should be taken. There is a section at the back of the book where you can keep notes of the case as it progresses through the court system, and a page where you can document the final resolution of the court.

Dear Reader, I truly value your participation in my case, and I hope this book will expand your awareness of how to protect yourself from libel.

Nancy Richmond

Fred Long Commits Libel

My name is Nancy Richmond and I am a writer and a certified genealogist. For me, those two occupations just seem to go together. As a result, I have written several historical biographies, using the same type of format that Laura Ingalls Wilder used in her 'Little House on the Prairie' series of books. My goal is to interest young readers in history, and many of my books have been used in grade school and junior high social study projects.

My New Year's Resolution for 2020 (a year which shall live in infamy) was to research and write a biography on William Cody Richmond Sr., who was a soldier in the Revolutionary War and who was my husband's 5th great grandfather.

Since William Richmond was already listed in my family tree page on Ancestry.com, I had accumulated a large amount of documentation on his life. I spent several months collecting additional information, then verifying it to make sure it was correct. The data bases that I used included military records, books by Ed Robinson and James H. Miller, and United States Census, Marriage, Death and Burial Records. I also researched many family tree records on Ancesty, Wikitree, Family Search and other genealogy sites for sources. Most importantly, I had a copy of William Richmond's own sworn testimony about his military service from an 1832 court hearing.

My book, "William Cody Richmond – Revolutionary War Soldier" was finished by April and went on sale at the end of the month. The company that publishes my books is a subsidiary of Amazon.com, and Amazon sells all of my books for them, both to individuals and other book stores online. My books are sold in many other countries and in several languages.

My husband and family members were all thrilled with the book, and it was inducted into the Library of Congress in Washington D.C. as an historical biography. Little did I know that its publication would lead to so much pain and confrontation in the coming year.

As a genealogist, I am a member of many family tree groups on face book. While checking the posts on the Summers County, WV Genealogy group later that year, I saw a post from a Mr. Fred Long, who I had never heard of until that day (although he may have posted in the group in the past and I missed his messages). Mr.

Long was advertising a new book he had written that was called "William Richmond and the Fortification of Fort Randolph Point Pleasant, WV". The post said that the Greenbrier Historical Society in Lewisburg had copies for sale.

    I was thrilled with the news and immediately drove to the North House Museum, home to the Greenbrier Historical Society, of which I am a member. Mr. Long's book was small, only 51 pages, and did not look as if it were professionally published. Still, I bought the book and hurried home to give it to my husband.

    You can imagine our dismay when

we read the introduction, which stated:

"Nancy Richmond, in her book, a dreamed up account of what she purports to be a biography of William Cody Richmond, as it relates to his military service, is a gross misrepresentation of the facts; facts that cannot be ignored by serious genealogists that believe that facts and history matter. I hope to correct her inaccurate account with this narrative. I therefore set before you the facts relating to the fortification of Point Pleasant......."

I can truthfully say that I have never been so shocked and hurt by anything. I did not know this man, and I had no idea why he had so hatefully libeled me in print by saying I had dreamed up the information in my book. I decided to contact the company that had published the book, to find out if they had edited it before publishing it, and if they had tried to confirm the libelous statement. I went to the title page of the book to get the name of the publishing company. I found this:

    New River Publishing

    818 Summers Street

    Hinton, WV 25951

I really wanted to talk to someone from the publishing firm before I confronted Fred Long. However, there was no listing for a

New River Publishing in the phone book, so I dialed the operator. They confirmed that they had no listing by that name.

Next, I went to several genealogy groups on face book and posted a query as to whether anyone knew the phone number of a business called New River Publishing which was located at 818 Summers Street in Hinton. No one that replied to my post had ever heard of such a business.

Confused, I went to the 'City of Hinton Government' group on face book and posted a query about the company. I spoke with City Manager Chris Meadows. I was given the number of the Hinton City

Hall (304-466-3255), who said they had no such business licensed in the town. The City Hall employee gave me the number of the West Virginia Secretary of State Office (304-558-6000) and told me to call them and they would be able to tell me if there was such an entity as New River Publishing doing business in the state.

I called, but the person I spoke with said there was no legal company by that name in West Virginia, and gave me the number of the Federal IRS Tax Office (1-800-982-8291). I was instructed to call and ask if someone was doing business in West Virginia as a Sole Proprietorship or

Limited Liability Company by the name of New River Publishing, in which case they would have an EIN (Employee Identification Number).

When I called the US IRS Tax Office, the person who answered checked all of the records and said that New River Publishing was not in their records. She said they would conduct an investigation, because it might indicate a case of fraudulent misrepresentation.

According to the website below, www.legalmatch.com/law-library/article/fraudulent-mispresenation.html, there are several different types of fraudulent misrepresentation. They include making a statement to another party that is clearly false, making a statement that is partly true (a half lie) that means part may be true and part false, omitting details in a way that creates false beliefs in another person's mind, or being silent on a subject or failing to disclose important information (especially when they are legally required to provide it).

 I was still confused about Fred Long's book, so I went back to face book and scanned some of the genealogy sites. A couple of people on the sites asked what I had found out about New River Publishing,

and I explained what the various offices had reported to me. Then I looked up Fred Long's face book page. It was public, so I was able to read some of his posts. One post was dated July 28. In it Mr. Long stated:
"My little book has been printed. It came off the press Friday and I got it yesterday. Larry Fox, in Hinton, did the printing. I'm including a photo of the front and back. I think Larry's staff did a first rate job".

I continued reading the thread on Fred Long's book and saw that he was offering his book for sale online. In one post he agreed to sell a copy, then said, "Forgot to put down my address. It's 818

Summers Street, Hinton, WV 25951."

That post cleared up the mystery of New River Publishing. It was not a business as his book had implied, it was Fred Long's home, and in my opinion was a fraudulent misrepresentation.

I immediately looked up Larry Fox on face book. His page listed him as being the owner of Fox Yearbooks in Hinton. I sent him a private message telling him about what Fred Long had said about me in his book and asking if he was aware of the libel. He sent me the following message.

"Nancy, We are an online publisher. Our services are offered worldwide but mostly in the US. We do not edit nor sensor products when orders are final and packaged for publication as was the case in Mr. Long's book. Sincerely yours, Larry Fox."

Now that I knew that this man, Fred Long, was having his books printed by Fox Yearbooks, I went back to the book I had bought from the Greenbrier Historical Society and read his 'About the Author' page. It stated that Mr. Long had lived in Hinton all his life and had written several other booklets and had worked at a number of different businesses in Hinton, West Virginia before he retired.

After reading his biography, I sent a message to Fred Long on face book, asking him why he had libeled me in his book. The only possible reason (this is just my personal opinion) that I could think of was that my book on the same subject had come out a few months before his, which had angered him and caused him to want to defame me and my research. I also asked him about his reason for using the term New River Publishing, which according to the government employees I had spoken to, could be seen as some type of fraud. I informed him I was familiar with local laws, since I was a retired Greenbrier

County Town Recorder and Municipal Court Judge. His response was immediate and terrible.

"You are so full of hogwash. Is saying you were a former municipal court judge supposed to make me shake in my boots? Your arrogant, petty, juvenile, narcissistic tantrum got my post kicked off the Summers County West Virginia Face book page because of your sleazy PLEASE READ nonsense. You can't even read. OPINION! You got an opinion? My opinion is that your book that you pass off as 'the historical biography of William Cody Richmond' is nothing but a 'dreamed up' 'gross misrepresentation' of his military service. Now put that in your corncob pipe and smoke it!"

I was stunned with Fred Long's reply. In my entire life I had never had anyone speak to me in such a manner. I have no idea what I could have done to make this person treat me so badly.

Evidently, however, the information I had related to Mr. Long about his 'New River Publishing' being misleading to the public had worried him, because on August 27 he created a new face book group called (you'll never guess) New River Publishing at 818 Summers Street, Hinton, WV 25951.

He explained the new group this way.

"A word About New River Publishing" This is what I call my hobby. I live on the New River, as many of you know, and when I decided to start a face book group and publish documents I've collected over the past 45 years this seemed to be the logical name. It created somewhat of a ruffle with a woman in Lewisburg (meaning me), that jumped to the erroneous conclusion that NEW RIVER PUBLISHING was the name of a company even though the word company is nowhere to be seen. So just to clear the air, this is my hobby."

I eventually made myself read Fred Long's book. In my opinion there were many errors in his account of William Cody Richmond's Revolutionary War service, which is documented by dozens of reputable historians.

In the fall I published a second book about my husband's ancestor "William Richmond Sr. (1752-1850) Historical Records" in which I compiled documents and sources to prove the information in my earlier book. One chapter addressed some of the mistakes in Fred Long's book.

I made a comment to Mr. Long on Ancestry, a genealogy website we both belong to, about the additional evidence in my second book. I referred him to the article, "Settlement and Conflict (1600-1799)" which is posted on the West Virginia Department of Arts, Culture and History web site, that contains many documented sources. Their research shows that Fort Savannah, where William Richmond was stationed, had been built by 1775, one of the things Fred disputes.

I also mentioned that I had seen his face book post stating that he considered himself to be merely a hobby writer, who simply liked to look up research and post it in his NEW RIVER PUBLISHING group.

I was surprised when Fred replied to my message on Ancestry, agreeing with me.

"I have been a writer for 35 years and have published countless historical essays. Collecting historical records has been my hobby for over 40 years". (Fred's group was only a week old at the time of this post, so I don't know where he posted them before that). "Anyway, I'm tired of this and won't be responding anymore. I have better things to do. But if you are a professional you will start being truthful and stop trying to defend your bruised ego by making up things about me."

I assumed from what Fred Long said

in his post I would not have any further dealings with him. Unfortunately, I could not have been more wrong.

Fred Long Claims Libel

The long hard months of 2020 finally ended, and I had not heard anything from Fred Long for some time. So I was very surprised when on January 6, 2021, I received a certified letter from a local attorney, John H. Bryan. Apparently, Fred Long had decided that I had libeled him in my second book and had hired a lawyer to sue me, even though I had taken no legal action over his obvious libel of me the year before.

Before you read any further, please let me explain that there are 4 elements that must be present in order for someone to prove they have been libeled or defamed, as stated at https://splc.org/2001/06/libel-law/

1. <u>Publication</u> – a statement that is communicated to anyone other than the person to whom the statement is about.

2. <u>Identification</u> – a statement which identifies the person you are talking about.

3. <u>Harm</u> – A statement is harmful only if it SERIOUSLY shames, ridicules, disgraces or injures a person's reputation or livelihood. . Statements that are merely embarrassing or inaccurate do not meet the 'harm' test.

4. <u>Fault</u> – In order to prove fault when publishing a statement, the person suing

another person must prove that the offender made a reasonable effort to verify the information before publishing it. (Something Fred Long made no effort to do before libeling me in his book, and something which I made every effort to do by talking to Fred, government agencies, and other people on social media before publishing the information in this book). Below is the letter I received from Attorney John Bryan on behalf of Fred Long.

John Bryan: "I have been retained by Fred Long in regards to actions which you have taken against him on social media, Ancestry.com, and in print publication.

Please forward any future documents or communications to my attention, rather than directly to my client".

My Response: I have done as Mr. Bryan requested, and have not communicated directly with Mr. Long since receiving this letter. Dear Reader, please be aware that a statement must be FALSE in order to be libel or defamation. Nothing I have said in this case was false. Also, my first amendment right, the freedom of speech, allows me to have an opinion or belief about any subject, even if the word opinion is merely implied.

John Bryan: "It has come to my attention that you have made numerous misrepresentations regarding Mr. Long's book, "William Richmond and the Fortification of Fort Randolph, Point Pleasant, WV." As you know, you recently published your book, "William Richmond Sr. 1752-1850" in which you wrote that "Although Mr. Long describes himself as a serious historian in the book's introduction, the many errors found in the book prove that he is not." You further claimed that Mr. Long made "broad generalizations that cannot be proven," including that he was somehow incorrect in referring to West Virginia as "West Virginia" and other false, defamatory allegations. You declared that Mr. Long provided no specific documentation for his claims in his book, which is wholly false. To the contrary, his book contains over 130 endnotes of specific documentation".

My Response: All of my statements were made as an historian and a certified genealogist, and are my professional opinions. Mr. Long made a literary gaffe, which was also incorrect in a literal sense, when he titled his book "William Richmond and the Fortification of Fort Randolph, Point Pleasant, WV". Other than a small replica fort built in recent years, there was never a Fort Randolph in the state of West Virginia. The fort that existed in the time period when

William Richmond Sr. was a soldier was located in the British Colony of Virginia, during a time of rebellion by its colonial citizens. That is a fact, not libel. As for the 130 end notes, they are very general in context and could be considered speculation by historians, not facts. Additionally, a debate about end notes does not meet the criteria for 'harm' in a libel suit.

John Bryan: "Moreover, you falsely claimed that Mr. Long provided no proof that Captain Arbuckle marched his men to Fort Pitt, rather than traveling directly to Point Pleasant. To the contrary, if you will review Mr. Long's book, you will notice that he indeed offered evidence that Arbuckle's company marched directly to Fort Pitt, prior to arriving at Point Pleasant. Such a route for the company would be consistent with Arbuckle obtaining supplies for the garrison at Fort Pitt, which would also allow transport via the Ohio River, using boats, directly to Point Pleasant where they built Fort Randolph. As you know, boats would allow for much great cargo capacity than would pack horses".

My Response: When Commander Arbuckle took the 3rd Regiment, of which William Richmond was a part, from Fort Savannah to Fort Randolph, he had two routes he could have taken. The first route, through the woods, would have involved a trip of 150 miles. The second, going in the opposite direction from Fort Randolph, would have been a trip of 300 miles. There is no record of William Richmond ever having been at Fort Pitt. More importantly, when William Richmond applied for his Revolutionary War pension at the Greenbrier County Courthouse in Lewisburg, Virginia in 1832, he made a sworn statement saying that he had MARCHED (not taken a boat) from Fort Savannah directly to Fort Randolph. This is a well documented FACT and the original document is stored at the Federal National

Archives, Record Group 29, Washington DC #9088.

John Bryan: "You also argue that Mr. Long was wrong about the possibility of William Richmond being present at the murder of Cornstalk at Fort Randolph in 1777. However, Mr. Long in-fact offered evidence of the same. Cornstalk was murdered on November 10, 1777. Richmond testified that he served two years and one month, beginning in October of 1775, which placed him in active militia service at the time. As you know, numerous members of Richmond's local militia units were garrisoned at Fort Randolph at the time the murder occurred, as evidenced by numerous records, including the narrative of John Stuart".

<u>My Response</u>: Mr. Long provided speculation, not fact. Just because William Richmond was based at Fort Randolph in October (he may have already been discharged if he originally enlisted on October 1st), it in no way proves he was physically present on the day of Cornstalk's murder. Richmond could have been on leave, he could have been out with a scouting party, or out hunting on that day. So it is a moot point, and I was giving my professional opinion to the matter. Many of

the supposed 'allegations' by Fred Long are known to be debatable, and as a result cannot be proven either true or false. Again, his claim does not meet the criteria for 'harm' in a libel suit.

<u>John Bryan</u>: "Additionally, you claimed that Mr. Long stated that William Richmond was stationed at Arbuckle's Fort, which is false. Rather, he stated that Richmond may have been stationed there, because John Stuart wrote a letter from Camp Union, dated August 10, 1776, which is now preserved in the Draper Manuscripts and has a copy. He wrote, "I expect to have a fort soon completed at Camp Union, large enough to

contain the greatest part of the inhabitants."
In Mr. Long's book this source was cited and documented in an end note".

<u>My Response:</u> It was my OPINION that Fred Long implied William Richmond was stationed at Fort Arbuckle. It is a FACT that Fred wrote, "Richmond saying, he wintered at Fort Savannah, now Lewisburg. He means that he wintered in that vicinity, not the actual fort because it wasn't built until the late summer and early fall of 1776". This is a false statement. Also, the same John Stuart who Mr. Long quoted also said in his book "Memoire of the Indian Wars and Other Occurences" when speaking of the

gathering of militia for the Battle of Point Pleasant, "It was assembled at Fort Savannah in Greenbrier about the 4th of September, 1774. In fact, Attorney Bryan, you have documents posted on your own face book page from November 27, 2018, taken from the West Virginia Department of Culture and History, where you state that "The date of the building of Fort Savannah ... 1770 is widely accepted". Even more importantly, there is sworn testimony that was given by the wife and son of Captain Mathew Arbuckle at the 1832 pension hearing of William Richmond at the Greenbrier County Courthouse in Lewisburg, Virginia. Both

Frances Arbuckle Welch and Charles Arbuckle swore that William Richmond's testimony that he was stationed at Fort Savannah in 1775 was true. The record is on file at the Federal National Archives, Record Group 29, Washington DC #9088.

John Bryan: "You furthermore alleged that Mr. Long paid someone to print his book, which is false".

My Response: My opinion on this matter comes from the fact that on face book on July 28, Fred Long posted on his page that "My little book has been printed. It came off the press Friday and I got it yesterday. Larry Fox, in Hinton, did the printing. I'm including a photo of the front and back. I think Larry's staff did a first rate job."

In August, Larry Fox sent me a private message which said, "Nancy, We are an online publisher. Our services are offered worldwide but mostly in the US. We do not edit or sensor products when orders are final and packaged for publication as in the case of Mr. Long's book. Sincerely yours, Larry Fox." It is my opinion that these two comments taken together indicate that Fred Long paid Larry Fox (in some fashion) for printing his books. The only other alternative would have to be that, in my opinion, Mr. Long used an different name when he paid to have his book printed (someone had to have paid the costs of printing since Mr. Long does not own a printing press.)

<u>John Bryan</u>: "You furthermore wrote on face book that, "Since the business (New River Publishing) is being advertised in a book, but is not a legal business entity, that is fraud which is a federal offense... "and also that (he) does not have a valid license or IRS tax number to do business in the state, making them illegal".

<u>My Response</u>: My comments on face book were my own personal opinion, and were only offered in order to answer questions

from members of face book which asked me what I was told when I contacted local, state and federal government offices (as I was told to do by a Hinton town council member) about whether New River Publishing was a legal business entity. I merely repeated the information I was given by the US IRS office. It is the truth that if Mr. Long is selling his books without a Resale Certificate, A Seller's Permit or a Vendor's Certificate of Authority, he is in violation of the LAW. The Law states that when you resell your books to your customers personally, you are obligated to pay sales tax to the state in which the transaction takes place. You are also required to fill out state tax forms and pay sales tax to the state. It is a fact that The Greenbrier Historical Society is selling books for Fred Long. My opinion is that he has not fulfilled the requirements set forth by the state to sell them. To do otherwise is against the law.

John Bryan: "In addition to the text of your recent book, you have made numerous defamatory statements on social media about Mr. Long and his book. These false statements, in addition to the aforesaid book, have directly damaged Mr. Long's reputation, and have caused him damages, for which he is entitled to recover under the law".

<u>My Response:</u> Since Mr. Long is retired and claims that his books are merely a hobby, not a business, then he cannot claim 'fault' which as you know is one of the 4 elements that must be proven for libel to have taken place. His ability to make money has not been affected by anything I have said or done, and as I am sure you are aware, statements that are mildly embarrassing or merely confusing or inaccurate do not meet the 'harm' test.

<u>John Bryan:</u> "Mr. Long has authorized me to file a lawsuit against you to pursue justice for these claims and to obtain damages for

the harm which has occurred and which continues to occur. However, in the interest of avoiding litigation, he will refrain from filing suit if you immediately withdraw your book, "William Richmond Sr. 1752-1850" from circulation and remove the chapter pertaining to Mr. Long prior to any additional publication or circulation.

Mr. Long also demands that you publicly acknowledge on every internet post where you claimed Mr. Long said William Richmond was stationed at Fort Arbuckle, this includes Ancestry.com, that Mr. Long did not, at any time, say that William Richmond was at any time stationed at

Arbuckle's Fort.

Mr. Long also demands that you publicly acknowledge on every internet post, including Ancestry.com, where you claimed Mr. Long's book has no documentation, that Mr. Long's book has in fact over one hundred and thirty endnotes documenting his findings and that you purposefully and willfully mischaracterized (Mr. Bryan's spelling) his book by saying he did not provide specific documentation.

Mr. Long also demands that you publicly acknowledge on every internet post that you commented on Mr. Long's newspaper article that you purposely and fraudulently claimed that Mr. Long said in the article that nothing of that nature was said or implied in the article.

Mr. Long demands that these corrections also be communicated to everyone who has obtained a copy of the original book containing the defamatory statements".

My Response: Any OPINIONS that I might have given on any social media do not meet the criteria for 'fault' which must be met in order to prove that Mr. Long was defamed by me in any way.

John Bryan: "Please provide proof of your compliance with these demands within fourteen (14) days of your receipt of this letter. Otherwise we will proceed with litigation. Please feel free to call me if you would like to discuss this matter in further detail. Very truly yours, John H. Bryan".

<u>My Response</u>: I have never made libel or defamatory statements about Fred Long on social media or anywhere else. As I have stated before, I am entitled to my own opinion under Constitutional Law. Everything else I have stated was either supplied to me by local, state and federal government agencies, or has been proven by sources I have provided. For libel to take place, a statement must be false, and I have

not said anything false about Mr. Long. In contrast, Mr. Long has libeled me many times, beginning with the statement in the introduction of his book in which he says I 'dreamed up' my book, although I posted dozens of sources.

In conclusion, Dear Reader, I would like to say that Attorney Bryan urged me to call him if I wanted to discuss this case. I called his office on several occasions, but was told he was not available. I emailed him, and gave him several dates that I would be home and available to take his call, but I never heard from him.

I would love to hear from YOU, however, and learn what your thoughts are on this case. Take care, and be mindful of what you say. There are con artists and criminals everywhere who are waiting to take advantage of you.

I have included some documentation to support the information I provided to Attorney John Bryan, that prove my statements to him in my earlier books on William Cody Richmond Sr. are true.

Lawsuit Documentation

Camp Union: By the mid 1700's, Virginia Colony had spawned a generation of hardy and independent citizens who were anxious to improve their situation by obtaining land of their own. The Greenbrier region along the western border of Virginia, through which the Greenbrier River flowed, became a mecca for many of the settlers moving onto the outskirts of the colony.

In her book, "Greenbrier Pioneers and Their Homes", well known historian Ruth Woods Dayton describes the area, saying, "The beautiful bluegrass plateau, or savannah, comprising an area of twenty miles in length and varying from two to five miles in width, bounded by Muddy Creek, Brushy Ridge, Butler Mountain, and the Greenbrier River, was long ago given the highly descriptive name of The Great Levels. While Andrew Lewis was making his survey in this region, he discovered, about 1751, a clear mountain spring of unusual size and volume, which for many years thereafter was known as 'Lewis Spring'. Located just miles west of the Greenbrier River, at the foot of a sloping elevation, it became a dominant factor in the growth of a little settlement which clustered around it and was known simply as Savannah".

The location of the spring soon became known to travelers, and families often spent weeks or months camped at the site while scouting the surrounding area for a good place in which to settle. The Virginia Colony Regular Army also made use of the spot, and referred to it as Camp Union in their military reports.

As word of the beautiful open savannah land in the Greenbrier Valley reached the coast, hundreds of colonists packed their belongings and moved to the border land, building homesteads without the permission of the Virginia authorities.

Their actions broke the terms of the British and French Treaty of Aix-la-Chapelle, which denied English colonists the right to use that portion of land between Ohio and Virginia.

The outraged French Canadian Governor sent an army of his soldiers and their Indian allies into the contested area, where they erected a series of lead plates on which a declaration asserting French ownership of the territory was inscribed. The French also made treaties with the Chiefs of many of the local Indian tribes, and encouraged them to drive the English settlers out of the valley. To further secure their rights, the French built a line of forts along the perimeter of the disputed land to deter British homesteaders from entering the territory.

The actions of the French angered Virginia's Governor Robert Dinwiddie. In retaliation he instructed one of his officers, George Washington, to deliver a directive to the French Commander at Fort Le Boeuf on the Allegheny River. The message, which stated that the French army was encroaching on British territory, left the French Commander unmoved.

In 1754, in an effort to demonstrate his resolve in the matter, Dinwiddie sent out two companies of soldiers to build a British fort on the river. When it was finished, George Washington and two companies of soldiers were ordered to march to the fort and protect it. Andrew Lewis was a Captain in Washington's regiment at that time and was one of his best men.

While they were still some miles from the river, a British scout arrived at Washington's camp at Great Meadows to warn him that the French had captured the British fort. But before he could react to the news, Washington's troops were surrounded by the French army.

A skirmish ensued, and the French Commander was killed. His men, who outnumbered the British troops three to one, forced Washington to surrender and made him promise not to build another fort in the area for at least one year. The agreement caused the Greenbrier Valley settlers to fear that they would be evicted from their homes, and as a result The Battle of Great Meadows heralded the beginning of the French and Indian War.

When Governor Dinwiddie heard rumors that the French planned to build a line of forts along the Greenbrier and New Rivers, he reacted quickly. On September 11, 1754, he ordered Andrew Lewis to take a company of men to the Greenbrier Valley to protect the colonial settlers, instructing the troops to 'repel Force by Force' against anyone who tried to harm or commit any hostile acts against the people in that area. Lewis agreed, but the winter was a hard one, and no attacks were made. As a result, the company under Lewis was recalled to Fort Cumberland in November.

In the spring of 1755, the settlers living along the Greenbrier River became hopeful when they learned the Governor had ordered two regiments of British Regulars to march to the border to combat the French. Led by General Edward Braddock, a force of more than fourteen hundred soldiers (aided by four hundred and fifty militiamen and a number of Indian scouts) marched toward the French stronghold.

On the ninth day of July, however, the party was ambushed and destroyed by French soldiers. General Braddock was among the casualties, and the British declared the mission a total failure.

That same summer, Andrew Lewis was sent to build two new forts in the Greenbrier district. It has never been proven that the forts were built, however, because Lewis and his company were constantly threatened by the French and by the Indian raiding parties that terrorized the countryside.

By August, Andrew Lewis and his men had returned to Fort Dinwiddie. As soon as their departure became known to Chief Cornstalk, he sent warrior bands called 'Flying Parties' onto the border.

These raids wreaked havoc on the unprotected settlers. The renegades killed at least seven persons, burned a dozen houses and killed or stole more than five hundred horses and cows. Around sixty people managed to make their way to a small stockade, where they were under siege for several days. By the time militia soldiers came to their rescue, the Shawnee had already returned to their villages.

The survivors of the attack were escorted to Fort Dinwiddie. The Governor displayed no sympathy for them. Instead he berated them, saying that they had displayed a 'shameful panic' by deserting unharvested crops and homesteads for the Indians to plunder. But no amount of urging could convince the frightened villagers to return to the Greenbrier Valley.

In February of 1756, Andrew Lewis headed an expedition of 340 men against the Shawnee tribes. Unfortunately, the endeavor was beset by heavy rain, flooded rivers, and a severe lack of supplies which eventually forced the men to turn back.

Finally, in 1758, General John Forbes attacked the French army at Fort Duquesne. The French soldiers were stretched to the breaking point at that time by their efforts to defend their enormous holdings, however, so Fort Duquesne was not prepared for the battle.

Rather than accept defeat, the French blew up the fort and retreated. As a result, the Indian tribes interpreted the departure as a sign of weakness on the part of the French, and made treaties instead with the British.

Although the Greenbrier Valley was

temporarily at peace, British officials in Virginia decided not to reopen the area for settlement. Their decision angered the Greenbrier Company and several other land speculators, who feared the loss of their grants. They began encouraging settlers to return to the Greenbrier district.

The speculators promised that the British government would soon begin awarding land grants to anyone who was already living in the territory. As a result, some foolhardy colonists heeded the bad advice and in 1761 moved into the lands around the Greenbrier River and Muddy Creek, setting up squatter's claims.

The Ottawa tribes, led by Chief Pontiac, soon learned of the new British settlements. They banded together with the other Indian nations and began to attack the homesteaders, pushing them back onto English occupied land.

In 1763, Shawnee Chief Cornstalk and sixty of his best warriors entered the border settlement at Muddy Creek under a flag of peace. Once they had been made welcome, the natives attacked and either killed or captured all of the inhabitants. The warriors then proceeded to the Savannah community near the Lewis spring, where they repeated their heinous atrocities.

Word of the vicious attacks reached the British government, who immediately issued an edict forbidding any English colonists to venture west of the crest of the Appalachian mountains, and ordering any settlers who had taken up residence beyond that point to return to British occupied land. Eventually the British ordered Colonel Henry Bouquet to assemble a large expedition of men and to march into the wilderness to negotiate peace treaties with the Mingo, Shawnee and Delaware tribes.

On September 10, 1764, Commander Andrew Lewis sent 150 militiamen to join the venture. The mission was a success, and all of the native tribes agreed to a cessation of hostilities. Charles Lewis, the brother of Andrew Lewis, was assigned the duty of finding and escorting any colonists who had been held prisoner by the natives to Fort Pitt on the Ohio River. Among them were many settlers who had been captured from the Greenbrier Valley over a ten year period. The French had been thwarted in their attempt to keep the British out of the Greenbrier Valley. As a result, many of the homesteaders from Savannah returned to their farms.

Fort Union: Soon after the French and Indian War ended, the British Secretary of State and Overseer of the American Colonies, Lord Shelburne, approved the opening of western Virginia for settlement by British colonists. The territory consisted of thousands of square miles of mountains, forests, and level savannahs that would make excellent homesteads.

All along the Greenbrier River, pioneers began carving out settlements. But the homesteaders had not forgotten the horrors of the French and Indian War and feared future attacks. As a result, forts became a way of life on the border.

According to historian Ruth Woods Dayton, there were three very different types of fortifications that were built in western Virginia during the 1700's. However, all three were referred to in reports and documents merely as forts.

The most simple type of frontier fort was a blockhouse. It was the smallest and easiest to build. A blockhouse was a square two-story building whose second story walls were wider than the bottom section of the structure. The upper portion of the building had narrow windows or portholes that could be used to shoot a firearm through in case of an attack.

The second style of fortification was a palisaded fort, also called a stockade. It was made up of a large two story log house surrounded by a fence that was ten or twelve feet high. The fence consisted of double rows of logs placed upright, and a heavy puncheon gate.

A military fort was the third and strongest of the border fortresses, and combined features of the other two types. Military forts were rectangular in shape. The interior walls of the fort were lined with cabins which joined palisades so as to form a stockade wall. The doors of the cabins all opened into a common courtyard.

Blockhouses were erected at the corners of the enclosure. In addition, some of the larger forts erected military barracks to house the soldiers that would be stationed there for long periods of time. This type of fort was used by the British army and by militia companies. It was also a meeting place for armed forces that were being assembled for an expedition.

Many of the farmers who lived at Savannah near the Lewis Spring earlier had already returned and rebuilt their burned homesteads. In 1770 a fort was erected just above the site of the spring. It was big enough to accommodate a large number of soldiers, since it boasted several barracks and four blockhouses, and could easily accommodate settlers during an attack.

The new stockade was called Fort Savannah by the colonists and local militia. However, the British army referred to it as either Camp Union or Fort Union until they lost control of the territory at the beginning of the Revolutionary War in 1775.

All along the Greenbrier River, homesteaders from the coast began carving out settlements. Colonel John Stuart founded Frankfort. Thomas Williams settled at what would become Williamsburg. William McKinney claimed land on Muddy Creek

Mountain. The Keeny family from the valley of Virginia built a small fort on Kenny's Knob. Two brothers, Jacob and Adam Mann, built a fort at the site of what would eventually become the town of Union in Monroe County. John McNeil and his family founded the town of Little Levels near the white sulphur springs. At the same time, Andrew Donnally built Fort Donnally near present day Alta.

   The confrontation that the settlers feared was not long in coming. Many of the local native tribes were angry because they thought that the British colonists were not honoring their treaty agreement to stay out of the lands south of the Ohio River. The Shawnee nation began recruiting other tribes to join with them in attacking the homesteaders. Renegades from the Mingo, Cherokee, Wyandotte, Miami, Delaware, and Wabash nations answered their appeals.

Early in 1773, a band of Shawnee warriors murdered George Yeager, a farmer whose homestead fronted the Elk River. Soon after, some settlers who were passing through the Greenbrier district to reach Kentucky under the leadership of Daniel Boone were waylaid by Indians. Five members of their party were killed, including Boone's own son. Those who survived retreated back east.

By 1774, most of the western tribes were in open rebellion against the settlers of the Greenbrier Valley. Unlike the more organized attacks that had been controlled by the French, small bands of renegade warriors traveled through the countryside at will, assaulting any homesteaders they came across; killing men, women and children and burning their homes. One raiding party attacked a small settlement at Cedar Grove, killing homesteader Walter Kelly and his young servant boy. The remainder of the inhabitants managed to escape to safety, but the village was lost.

Infuriated by the attacks, the local frontiersmen began making raids of their own into Indian territory. Not knowing which natives were making the assaults against the Greenbrier homesteaders, they sometimes killed members of friendly tribes, further inflaming the hostilities.

That summer Indians attacked a group of militiamen who were under the command of Captain John Dickenson near the Greenbrier River. Several of the men were badly wounded and one was killed. Around the same time, Arbuckle's Fort at Muddy Creek was fired on. In July one of the survivor's of an earlier massacre at

Cedar Creek was killed and his young daughter was taken hostage.

In the fall of 1774, the British authorities issued a letter of warning to the colonial militia, telling them to expect an imminent attack by the natives, and to prepare to repel their advance. The frontiersmen of the Greenbrier Valley interpreted the letter to be a declaration of war against the renegades. They dubbed the conflict Cresap's War in memory of a group of surveyors who had been attacked by Indians earlier that year.

Rather than wait for an assault, some of the men raided a nearby Mingo village.

They killed the family of Chief Logan, who was friendly with the local homesteaders. Their actions further inflamed the native war parties to attack the settlers.

Lord Dunmore, the Governor of Virginia Colony, ordered General Andrew Lewis to have his men build a fort on the Kanawha River as a base of operations, and to then destroy all of the Indian villages in the area. Next, the Governor called for the creation of a large expeditionary force of soldiers to combat the Indian threat. He ordered them to meet at what would later become Lewisburg.

Years later, Revolutionary War

Colonel John Stuart wrote in his book, "Memoire of the Indian Wars and Other Occurrences" about the meeting, saying, "It was assembled at Fort Savannah in Greenbrier about the 4th of September, 1774".

Historian Ruth Woods Dayton agreed with Stuart in her book "Greenbrier Pioneers and Their Homes", when she wrote about the existence of Fort Savannah before the battle of Point Pleasant, saying, "One feels justified in stating it was standing at that time and that it must have been of fair size, at least with a stockade enclosure. Otherwise Lord Dunmore would almost certainly have chosen as a meeting place one of the other logs forts that were available in different sections of the region. A shelter for the protection of flour, ammunition, and other supplies, as well as an enclosure for the cattle and horses, would have been an essential consideration in the selection of the location of the army rendezvous".

Additional documentation of Fort Savannah was provided by historian Virgil A. Lewis when he wrote of the battle: "On the return of General Lewis's army from Dunmore's War {in 1774}, William Kennerly, a sergeant of Captain George Mathew's Company of Augusta County men, was left with a garrison numbering fifteen men at Fort Savannah".

Lord Dunmore's call to arms was answered by hundreds of frontiersmen from the Greenbrier Valley and beyond. The militiamen all had the desire to rid their homeland from the constant threat of invasion. They gathered at Fort Savannah, awaiting orders from the militia officers and British commanders. Many years later President Theodore Roosevelt, when he spoke about the men who came together at Fort Savannah, was quoted as saying,
"It may be doubted if ever a braver or physically finer set of men were ever got

together on this continent".

Dunmore sent a post to General Andrew Lewis instructing him to march the militiamen to the Kanawha River in order to rendevous with him and the British Regular Army there. Lewis set out from Fort Savannah in September, with a band of men numbering eleven hundred. The 160 mile route was charted by Capt. Mathew Arbuckle, an able bodied scout who knew the territory well.

The army made slow progress, since there were no roadways wide enough to accommodate such a large brigade of soldiers and its supply train of wagons, pack horses and cattle. An experienced corp of ax men headed the expedition, chopping trees and widening paths so the army could pass through the heavily forested wilderness. Arbuckle's route led the colonial forces over Muddy Creek Mountain, Meadow Creek, Walker's Creek and Buffalo Branch before turning northwest toward what is now Ansted.

The company made slow progress because of the large number of men and animals involved, so it was many days before the militia arrived at the confluence of the Kanawha and Ohio Rivers. General Lewis had expected to join with Dunmore and his troops when they reached Point Pleasant. But a British courier was waiting at the Point to inform the General that Dunmore and his army had already crossed the river into Ohio and built a fort at the mouth of the Hocking River.

The messenger also stated that Dunmore was presently on route to the Pickaway Plains, and had ordered Lewis to meet him there with his troops. After agreeing to do so, Lewis told his men to make camp for the night.

General Lewis had no idea that the Shawnee Chief Cornstalk and over one thousand warriors had been tracking the soldiers and had surrounded their base. Cornstalk, believing it would be easier to defeat the militia before it could reunite with the British Regulars, planned to attack the campsite at dawn.

In what was a stroke of luck for the Virginians, several men left the camp just before dawn to go foraging for food. When they entered a meadow near the river, the men saw before them what seemed to be an uncountable number of Indian braves, which covered about five acres of land. The warriors opened fire, but fortunately one soldier managed to escape and warn the militia of the impending attack.

The company drums began to beat, sounding the alarm for the soldiers to prepare for battle. When the Indians charged, two groups of about one hundred and fifty men rushed to the head of the company to meet the attack. The fight took place over a one mile front, with the opponents always in sight of each other.

The militia pressed ever forward, and the Shawnee began to retreat. The desperate confrontation lasted until well past noon, when the savages took cover in the forest and finally disappeared into the trees, carrying their dead and wounded with them. Sporadic firing continued until about eleven o'clock that evening, after which only the moaning of wounded men from both sides could be heard.

When the Battle of Point Pleasant ended, the militia casualties numbered almost one fifth of their forces, and the enemy deaths were much higher. Many men from the Greenbrier Valley, including Thomas McClung, who lived on Muddy Creek Mountain, had been killed.

General Lewis sent a dispatch to Governor Dunmore with details of the battle. Two days later an answer arrived, ordering the militia to join Dunmore's army in Chillicothe so that they could combine forces and pursue the enemy.

Leaving the camp and the wounded soldiers under the command of one of his officers, Lewis and the men who could still fight headed off to meet Dunmore and the British troops. Before they could reach the Shawnee villages in Ohio, however, Lord Dunmore and his men had already met with Chief Cornstalk and several other Chiefs who were anxious to sue for peace.

Dunmore had his soldiers set up a temporary headquarters, Camp Charlotte, where he could treat with the other Chiefs. He sent world to General Lewis to leave his slow moving army and come with all haste to the negotiations. However, Lewis feared his army would attack the natives on sight if he was not present, so he decided against leaving them.

Similarly, the natives were worried that the militia would burn their villages as they passed by, so they positioned warriors along the river bank to prevent that from happening. As a result, it was only with great difficulty that Lewis was able to restrain the angry frontiersmen from firing on their opponents. Even after they reached Camp Charlotte, General Lewis had to post triple guards around the perimeter of the camp to ensure that his men would not kill any of the Chiefs.

On the twentieth day of October, the Treaty of Camp Charlotte was signed. The terms of the agreement stated that the Indian tribes that had been involved in the insurrection would no longer hunt in the area that had been opened for colonial settlement by the British government, and that they would return any captives and horses that had been taken in the raids of the past two years. Each of the Chiefs had to agree to turn over members of their tribes to be held as hostages by Dunmore, to prove their sincerity in keeping the treaty.

The West Virginia Department of

Culture and History confirms in the article below that Fort Savannah was already in existence at the time the Battle of Point Pleasant took place. {Taken from the website at www.wvculture.org.}

'Exploration, Settlement and Conflict'

{1600-1799}

FORT   SAVANNAH

" A most important military post located on the site of Lewisburg, Greenbrier County, presumably between 1769 and 1774. It was the meeting point for the Virginians who marched under General Andrew Lewis to Point Pleasant in the fall of 1774. Some authorities suggest that a fort may have been erected on this site as early as 1755, under orders issued by General Braddock. By 1770, a fortified encampment called Fort Savannah was established at the Lewis Spring".

Sources for the article from the West Virginia Department of Culture and History are below.

Withers, Chronicles of Border Warfare,. pp.173, 209, 211-216, 227,241-243, 291.

De Hass, History of the Early Settlement and Indian Wars of Western Virginia,. pp. 154-159, 170-174.

Howe Historical Collections of Western Virginia,. p.366.

Thwaites, Reuben Gold, ed,. Documentary History of Dunmore's War,1774,. Madison WS, 1905., Compiled from the Draper Manuscripts, Library of the Wisconsin Historical Society. pp. 47,62,86,308-310.

Virginia Historical Register, Vol. 1, p.33.

Southern Literary Messenger, No. 1, Vol XIV, (1848) p. 26.

Fort Savannah: Even though the settlers in the Greenbrier Valley were thankful that treaties had been reached with the various native tribes following the Battle of Point Pleasant, a feeling of unease was pervasive throughout the Virginia Colony. The issue of taxation without representation in the British Parliament had sparked protests and boycotts among the colonists.

Several patriot groups had formed and rebelled against British rule. One such group, called The Sons of Liberty, threw a shipload of tea that had just arrived from England into the Boston Harbor in order to demonstrate their anger about unfair taxes.

The British retaliated against the colonists by closing down the harbor.

In desperation, the Americans held the First Continental Congress in the city of Philadelphia on October 26, 1774. During the Congress, the delegates organized an economic boycott against Great Britain and petitioned the King to address their many grievances. When he refused to negotiate, a Second Continental Congress was held in the spring of 1775, not long after the Revolutionary War began. Initially, the newly created Congress functioned as a de facto national government by directing strategy, appointing diplomats, and making formal treaties with other governments.

The Continental Congress also took control of the military efforts of the Americans in their revolt against the British Crown by forming the Continental Army. George Washington was chosen to be Commander-In-Chief, and served during the war without any compensation except for reimbursement of his expenses.

The army was organized into three divisions, six brigades, and thirty-eight regiments. The officers of the army were typically wealthy gentlemen farmers who had voiced an ideological commitment to opposing British rule. In contrast, the enlisted men came from the working class.

Most of the settlers were patriotic, and all able bodied men were motivated to volunteer in the newly formed army by specific contracts which entitled them to good wages, food, clothing and medical care; and the promise of land ownership after the war. At the onset of the conflict, soldiers agreed to serve in the army for a standard enlistment period of one year.

Fort Savannah, which became the official name of the military stockade at the Lewis Spring when the Continental Congress took control of Virginia, soon became one of the largest fortifications on the Virginia frontier. Unfortunately, the number of men available to serve at Fort Savannah had been drastically reduced after the British soldiers stationed there were withdrawn.

Homesteaders living along the Greenbrier River began to fear attacks by the local Shawnee and Mingo tribes. They sent letters to Commander-in-Chief George Washington, asking him to provide protection for border settlements. In response, many new recruits were sent to serve at Fort Savannah for their first one year term of service. Among them was William Richmond, who was born in Pennsylvania in 1752, and relocated to western Virginia in the spring of 1775.

When William learned that the Continental Congress had issued a call to arms, he reported to the local recruiting facility and took the Virginia Oath of Allegiance, which was required of all adult men in the state. The Oath helped the American government to determine the strength of the patriotic movement and to identify loyalists {colonists that supported British rule}. In taking the oath, William pledged to serve the state, and repeated,

"I do swear that I renounce and refuse all allegiance to George the Third, King of Great Britain, his Heirs and Successors, and that I will be faithful and bear true allegiance to the Commonwealth of Virginia, as a free and independent state, and that I will not, at any time, do, or cause to be done, any matter or thing that will be prejudicial or injurious to the freedom and independence thereof, as declared by Congress; and also, that I will discover and make known to some justice of the peace for the said state, all treasons or traitorous conspiracies which I now or hear after shall know to be formed against this or any of the United States of America."

By swearing the oath, William and the other men knew that they were guilty of treason against England, and would be subject to death by hanging if America lost the war. Few men were deterred.

According to military records {number S9088} at the Federal National Archives, William Richmond enlisted in the Continental Army in the spring of 1775 under Lieutenant Woods in the county of Botetourt. He served in the 3rd Virginia Regiment of the line under the following named officers: Captain Mathew Arbuckle and Colonel Neville. His first enlistment was for a one year period. William Richmond, according to the Archives, marched from Botetourt to Fort Savannah in the summer of 1775 and was stationed there throughout the winter under Captain Mathew Arbuckle.

In the spring of 1776, William Richmond's company marched to Point Pleasant on the Ohio River, under the command of Colonel Neville. Once there, the company helped to build and fortify Fort Randolph. William served at Point Pleasant until his enlistment ended.

Richmond's service record is fully documented in the military and civil courts of Virginia. It provides absolute proof for the existence of Fort Savannah, and that it had been built and was in use by the Continental Army in 1775.

Fort Savannah, according to

compiled documentation in the book "William Richmond Sr. {1752-1850} Historical Records", was a large military fort which had a sixty foot stockade fence. The fence was twelve feet high and it surrounded the encampment. The book provides a detailed description of Fort Savannah in 1775, and is well documented from numerous verified historical sources.

"Bastions for sentries were located on each wall. A large gate made from heavy slabs of wood was built on a rise above the Lewis Spring, which supplied water to the fort. Several small cabins that were located along the stockade walls opened into the courtyard. There were two militia barracks which provided housing for the soldiers. The fort was not only a place of defense, but was also a residence for a number of families who sheltered there whenever Indians or British troops were sighted in the area. There was a blacksmith shop and several barns where cattle, horses and chickens were kept. Altogether, the interior looked more like a small village than a military base".

    Sources from the book also confirm that William Richmond served a one year term at Fort Savannah. He then marched to Point Pleasant with his company along the same route taken by the colonial militia when they fought at the Battle of Point Pleasant in 1774. {As recorded in various military records, journals and letters written by soldiers who also served in Richmond's company that are posted on ancestry, wikitree and many other online genealogical sites. These documents consistently state that the trip to Point Pleasant took the men of the 3rd Virginia Regiment past Muddy Creek, Meadow Creek, Laurel Creek, Gauley Mountain, Cabin Creek and to the mouth of the Elk River}.

Author Ruth Woods Dayton stated concerning Fort Savannah in her book,

"Greenbrier Pioneers and Their Homes": "There is one fact that is virtually certain: the fort was in existence at the period of Lord Dunmore's War in the 1770's".

Additional verification is recorded by the highly respected historian Henry Howe in his book, "Virginia, Its History and Antiquities", published in 1945, which says: "The old Fort at this place stood about one hundred yards southeast of the site of the present courthouse, on land now belonging to Mr. Thomas B. Reynolds and the widow of Mr. William Mathews. It was erected about the year 1770".

On page thirty-one of her book

"Greenbrier Pioneers and Their Homes", Ruth Woods Dayton related the details of a Shawnee attack on Fort Donnally and its subsequent rescue by a group of sixty-six soldiers led by Colonel John Stuart from Fort Savannah as proof of the fort's existence during the Revolutionary War.

"It {Fort Savannah} was certainly standing at the time of the attack on the outpost fort at Andrew Donnally's. Colonel Stuart apparently utilized it then for the mustering of his relief company".

<u>Lewisburg</u>: By 1782, a preliminary peace treaty was signed between the Americans and the British. The agreement assured that

the Revolutionary War was nearing an end.

According to historian Ruth Woods Dayton, upon hearing of the peace treaty, the residents of the rapidly growing settlement of Fort Savannah petitioned to have their settlement be given a town charter. They 'by common agreement' named the town Lewisburg, in honor of General Andrew Lewis, who had first discovered the Lewis Spring and who had been a General during the Revolutionary War.

That same year the Virginia Assembly passed an Act that created the town of Lewisburg, with the following eight men listed as the original trustees – Samuel Lewis, James Reid, Samuel Brown, Andrew Donnally, John Stuart, Archer Mathews, William Ward, and Thomas Edgar. William Ward was named sheriff and later became High Sheriff of the town, while William Renick, John Anderson, James Alexander, George Clendenin and Samuel McClung became Justices for Greenbrier County.

The Act additionally specified that Lewisburg was to be laid out in a forty acre square that contained 'convenient streets'. The lots were to be half an acre each in size, and were to be sold at public auction.

One of the trustees, Thomas Edgar,

was also a surveyor. He laid out the map for the town. The trustees thought that Lewisburg should have wide, easily accessible roadways, because it was a crossroads for the old Midland and Seneca Trails that had been used for decades by anyone passing through the region, and were still heavily traveled.

It was decided by the trustees at that time to demolish Fort Savannah in order to accommodate the newly formed town. Early Lewisburg resident Marcellus Zimmerman, who was a prolific writer and newspaper man in the 1800's, often told the story that a pile of logs which still existed in the town when he was a boy were all that was left of Fort Savannah, whose walls had been torn down and used to build many of Lewisburg's first homes.

The most recognized building in the town was the Old Stone Presbyterian Church, which was built in 1796. {The Old Stone Church is the oldest church building west of the Allegheny Mountains that has remained in continuous use for over 200 years}. Land for the Church was donated by Colonel John Stuart. It was Stuart himself who chiseled into one of the building stones of the church the following inscription: "This building was erected in the year

1796 at the expense of a few of the first inhabitants of this land, to commemorate their affection & esteem for the Holy Gospel of Jesus Christ. Reader, if you are inclined to applaud their virtues, Give God the Glory".

The first school erected in the town was the Academy, established in 1808 by Reverend Dr. John McElhenney, who was also the instructor. The Academy was the first brick building built in Lewisburg, and the school was very successful.

Because Lewisburg was located on two well traveled roadways, the need for Taverns and Inns soon became evident. Several such establishments were built very early in the town's existence, and remained in operation for many years.

The Old Bell Stand, which was located on LaFayette Street, was one of the first Inns to be constructed. It was host to the Secretary of State Henry Clay in 1826.

The Star Tavern was also a popular Inn. It was built around 1820 as a home for John A. North, and later sold to James Frazier, who turned it into a tavern.

Other well known establishments operating near Lewisburg included the Tavern at the Bridge, which was located between Lewisburg and the Greenbrier River, and the Tuckwiller Tavern, which was opened at the edge of town.

The most famous of the Lewisburg Inns was built on Washington Street. The General Lewis Inn, named for General Andrew Lewis, is still in operation today. It is located along the section of U.S. Route 60 that runs through Lewisburg.

Every year, hundreds of families come from all over the United States to stay at the old hotel; which exudes an aura of southern gentility and charm. Many visitors claim that upon entering the lobby of the General Lewis Inn, they feel as if they have been transported back through time to the 18th century.

The General Lewis Inn originally was a brick home which was owned by Mr. John Withrow. When he died, the property was inherited by his daughter, Lettie Ford. She later sold the Inn to a hotel corporation, who added more sections to the building.

Mr. Randolph Hock, who was one of the original managers of the Inn, spent several years acquiring antiques from around Greenbrier County to add to the decor of the building. Antique poster beds, hand made quilts, cupboards, chest of drawers, china sets, oil lamps, original paintings and other period pieces set the establishment apart and made it a travel destination in its own right.

One of the oldest buildings in Lewisburg, known as 'Stuart Manor', was built and owned by Colonel John Stuart, who is known as the 'founder and father of Greenbrier County'. John Stuart has been described, according to Greenbrier County historian Ruth Woods Dayton, as 'a wiry, dark-eyed Scottish man of more than ordinary cultivation, a fearless hunter and a brave soldier'.

The Manor house was built near the county clerks office in Lewisburg. It was a two story house constructed of native limestone, and described as being 'somewhat

English' in character. The house was added to at regular intervals over the years, and it eventually had a total of fourteen outside doors. The windows all had solid battened shutters, which were popular at that time.

The Stuart family commonly chiseled their names on the outside stone walls of the Manor to commemorate important events. One such inscription read "This house was built in 1789'". Another said "J. Stuart 1807'", the year Colonel Stuart retired.

One of the first government buildings to be commissioned for the town was a stone structure that was used as a jail and also as the home of the jailer. At that time the town rarely had prisoners, so a basement area under the building, which was accessible by a trapdoor in the floor, was deemed to be an adequate place for criminals. In addition to a jail, a court order in 1793 allotted twenty dollars to be provided to the sheriff so that he could have a set of 'stocks' built to help control unruly citizens.

Just as necessary was a courthouse. A log house was originally used for that purpose, until it was deemed too small. It was replaced in 1800 by a large three story stone structure near Jefferson Street, which became known as the Old Stone Courthouse. Because of its size and its accessability, and because Lewisburg was the Greenbrier County Seat, the building was used by many courts in the state, including the Supreme Court of Virginia.

In 1832, a most fortuitous hearing took place at the Greenbrier County Old Stone Courthouse that provided absolute proof that Fort Savannah was constructed between 1770 and 1774. That evidence came as a result of the Revolutionary War Pension Application of William Richmond Sr., who was stationed at Fort Savannah during 1775 and 1776.

Although an earlier Pension Act was passed in 1828, it excluded many of the

Revolutionary War Veterans who had not been officers. In contrast, the Service-Pension Act that was passed on June7, 1832, included every officer or enlisted man who had served for at least two years in the Continental Line or State Troops, volunteers or militia; and also made them eligible for a pension for life.

Unlike the earlier legislation, the Act of 1832 did not require the applicants to demonstrate need in order to be eligible for the funds. Additionally, under the new Act, money due from the last payment until the date of death for the pensioner could also be collected by his widow or by his children.

William Richmond Sr. was 80 years old when the Act of 1832 was passed. He was not sure how to go about applying for his pension. It had been more than 50 years since he served in the Continental Army, and he had no documentation to prove his military service.

William eventually contacted the pension board, who explained the process to him. He then applied for his pension, and found witnesses who were willing to testify in court that he was a soldier at Fort Savannah in 1775..

Richmond's pension hearing took place at the Old Stone Courthouse in

Greenbrier County, Virginia, on October 22, 1832. A certified copy of the hearing was sent to the Virginia State Pension Records Department in Richmond, Virginia. The original document is now stored at the Federal National Archives, Record Group 29, Washington D.C. #S9088.

Copies of the record are also on file in the Military Fold 3 Records Division and in other historical record departments, and are available to the public. A transcribed copy of the hearing is documented below:

"State of Virginia

Greenbrier County

On this 22nd day of October, 1832,

appeared before the County Court of Greenbrier, it being a court of record – William Richmond Sr., a resident of Fayette County and state of Virginia, aged 80 years who first being duly sworn according to the law, doth on his oath make the following declaration in order to obtain the benefit of the provisions made by the Act of Congress passed on June 7, 1832. That he enlisted in the Army of the United States in the year 1775 with Lieutenant Woods and served in the 3rd Virginia Regiment of the line under the following named officers to wit: Capt. Mathew Arbuckle, Lieutenant Andrew Wallace, Col. Neville.

That he entered the service by enlisting under Lieut. Woods in the county of Botetourt, and State of Virginia for the term of one year in the month of Oct. 1775 and was marched from the county of Botetourt to the Savannah Fort {now Lewisburg} and was stationed there for some time under Capt. Mathew Arbuckle where the company wintered, and in the spring of 1776 he was marched to the fort at Point Pleasant on the Ohio River and was there stationed under the Command of Col. Neville. And there served out the time of his enlistment.

During his enlistment he was in no

engagement. And after his time in service was out, he again enlisted for another year under Capt. Arbuckle & Col. Neville and continued in the service at Point Pleasant and stationed as usual at the Fort of that place and continued service until his time of enlistment expired, and that he volunteered for one month to go with Capt. Arbuckle against the Indians but not getting a sufficient number of men, the expedition was abandoned.

And after being in the service one month was discharged and that the whole time of his service was two years & one month, that during that time he was in service he was in no Battle, that he was discharged from the service of his two years enlistment he thinks in the fall of 1777 and from his one month service as a volunteer in Nov. And following that he received written discharge and keeping the same for a number of years thinking it was of no value he gave the same to a step-son to play with and had good reason to believe the same has been lost.

That he herewith submits the evidence of Capt. Charles Arbuckle, son of said Capt. Mathew Arbuckle as evidence of his service & he hereby relinquishes every claim whatever to a pension or annuity

EXCEPT the present and he declares that his name is not on the pension roll of any agency in any state. Sworn to and subscribed the day and year afforsaid. William Richmond (X) his mark"

The court then presented the sworn testimony of witnesses Charles Arbuckle (son of Captain Mathew Arbuckle) and Frances Arbuckle Welch (wife of Captain Mathew Arbuckle). Both witnesses verified the information under oath that had been documented in William Richmond Senior's earlier claim, namely that he was stationed at Fort Savannah in 1775 and that he marched by land to Fort Randolph in 1776.

Their testimonies were sworn to and subscribed on the day and year aforesaid by Henry Erskine, Justice of the Peace.

Finally, William Richmond Sr. was called to the stand and presented his sworn statement before the judge and the court, in which he stated the following information.
"I, the undersigned William Richmond, give the following statement of my age & Revolutionary War Service.
To wit:

I was born in Pennsylvania in 1752. I settled in the county of Botetourt in the year of 1775 and in the same year I enlisted under one Samuel Wood, Lieut. We marched to Greenbrier and joined Capt. Mathew Arbuckle and Col. Neville. Our commissioners name was Ben Harris. We were marched to Point Pleasant, Ohio River. When I served out my term of two years and was discharged, I was kept in the service one month after my term was out. I got my discharge from Capt. Arbuckle in Lewisburg after my return. Since lost. I have never got my pension. In witness, I hereby attach my name.

X {William Richmond}"

The claim made by William Richmond Sr. in Lewisburg in 1832 was investigated by the United States Board of

Pension Applications and was found to be accurate. William was granted his pension by the board and was awarded a semi-annual allowance of $40.00 for the rest of his life.

William Richmond was one of the few Revolutionary War soldiers who lived long enough to have a photograph made before his death. He lived until 1850, when he died at the age of 98.

As a result of the pension hearing of William Richmond Sr. that was held at the Old Stone Courthouse on October 22, 1832, the existence of Fort Savannah in 1775 has been positively researched and verified.

That verification, in turn, has allowed the history of the town of Lewisburg to be accurately documented and preserved for future generations.

Bibliography

Chalkey, Lyman., Chronicles of the Scotch-Irish in Virginia., Extracted from the Original Court Records of Augusta County, 1745-1800., 3 Volumes., Rosslyn, VA. Mary Lockwood, 1912.

Cole, J. R., History of Greenbrier County.

DeHaas, Wills., History of the Early Settlement of West Virginia.

Dinwiddie, Robert., Official Records of Vols I, II, Virginia Historical Society.

Dayton, Ruth Woods., Greenbrier Pioneers and Their Homes., The West Virginia Historical Education Foundation Inc.,

Charleston, WV.1994.

Federal National Archives., Record Group # 29, National Archives, Washington, DC.

Fleming, William., Journal and Orderly Book, Documentary History of Dunmore's War., The National Historic Society. 1981.

Foote, Rev. Wm. H., Sketches of Virginia, Historical and Biographical.

Fry, Rose W., Recollections of the Rev. John McElhenney, D. D., Richmond: Whittet & Shepperson, 1893.

Hale, John P., Trans-Alleghany Pioneers.

Howe, General Henry.,Virginia, Its History and Antiquities., 1845.

Kercheval, Samuel., A History of the Valley

of Virginia., 4th Edition.

Lewis, Virgil A., Biennial Report of the State Historian and Archives.,1906.

McBride, Stephen W., Frontier Defense – Colonizing Contested Areas in the Greenbrier Valley of West Virginia., West Virginia Humanities Council.

McClung, Rev. William., McClung Genealogy., 1904.

Rice, Otis K., A History of Greenbrier County., 1986

Richmond, Nancy., Thomas McClung At The Battle of Point Pleasant., Richmond Books., 2015.

Greenbrier Map of Forts., from the Estate of

John Byrnside, https://scavengeology .com/last-will-and-testament-of-john-byrnside-1763-1816-2nd-white-child-born-in-monroe-county-west-va/.

Richmond Genealogy documentation., from http://freepages.rootsweb.com/~rlylebrown/genealogy/biorich.html

Richmond, Nancy., William Cody Richmond - Revolutionary War Soldier., Richmond Books., 2020.

Richmond, Nancy (compiled by).,William Richmond Sr. (1752-1850) Historical Records. Kindle Direct Publishing., 2020.

Renick, Sharelle., Attack on Fort Donnally., West Virginia Division of Culture and

History., at http://www.wvculture.org.

Stuart, John., Memoir of Indian Wars and Other Occurrences., Richmond Virginia Historical Society., 1833.

Thwaites, Reuben and Louise Phelps Kellogg., Documentary History of Dunmore's War., compiled from Draper Manuscript of 1774; published by Wisconsin Historical Society.

Waddell, James A., Annals of Augusta County (1726-1872)., Second Edition.

Wayland., John W., Virginia Valley Records.

Third Virginia Regiment Flag:
http://srvirginia.org/the-3rd-virginia-regiment-flag .

Court Case Notes

Court Case Notes

Court Case Notes

Court Case Notes

Final Case Resolution

www.ingramcontent.com/pod-product-compliance
Lightning Source LLC
Chambersburg PA
CBHW071409210526
45465CB00001B/309